Icarus Burning

New Women's Voices Series, No. 151

poems by

Hiromi Yoshida

Finishing Line Press
Georgetown, Kentucky

Icarus Burning

New Women's Voices Series, No. 151

*For Aaron,
upon whose disheveled
angel head green
accolades fall.*

Copyright © 2020 by Hiromi Yoshida
ISBN 978-1-64662-260-3 First Edition
All rights reserved under International and Pan-American Copyright Conventions. No part of this book may be reproduced in any manner whatsoever without written permission from the publisher, except in the case of brief quotations embodied in critical articles and reviews.

ACKNOWLEDGMENTS

Grateful acknowledgment is made to the editors of these publications in which these poems first appeared, sometimes in different versions.

Bathtub Gin, "Icarus Burning"
Borderline, "Speaking for Edvard Munch's *The Sin*"
Flying Island, "Kroger"
Indiana Voice Journal, "Menstruation at Fifty," "Lazarus," "IN v. LDS"
The Rain, Party, & Disaster Society, "The Abortion," "The Iconization of Rosa Parks," "Icarus Redux"
Tipton Poetry Journal, "The Ragdoll"
Work Literary Magazine, "The Exotic Dancer," "Porcelain Lady," "Life Drawing"

Publisher: Leah Maines
Editor: Christen Kincaid
Cover Art: *The Flight of Icarus,* Copyright 2019 by Louis Parsons (www.louisparsons.com)
Author Photo: Toyoko Yoshida
Cover Design: Elizabeth Maines McCleavy

Order online: www.finishinglinepress.com
also available on amazon.com

Author inquiries and mail orders:
Finishing Line Press
P. O. Box 1626
Georgetown, Kentucky 40324
U. S. A.

Contents

Icarus Burning 1
On the Prowl in the East Village 3
The Exotic Dancer 4
The Abortion 6
Menstruation at Fifty 8
Hot Flashing 9
Porcelain Lady 10
The Exotic Dance Club Patron 11
The "Four Stages of Eroticism" (Eve, Helen, Mary, Sophia) 13
Bivalve 15
Realia 16
The Iconization of Rosa Parks 17
Life Drawing 18
Speaking for Edvard Munch's *The Sin* 19
Lazarus 20
Kroger 21
The Doll 22
Duck, Duck, Goose 23
"Wanted" 24
Grandma and the Devil 25
Lily of the Valley 27
The Rejected Daffodil 28
IN v. LDS 29
#MeToo 31
The Ragdoll 32
Piano Burning 33
Icarus Redux 34
Additional Acknowledgments 35
About the Author 36

Icarus Burning

The Aztec heart of the sun blazes a rush hour trail of amniotic blood
        across skyscraping altars of plexiglass horizons

shimmering in the golden crucible of salt-licked Red Seatides
and questions pickled in formaldehyde jars

X-rated carbon copies of bones bleaching on perforated clotheslines

twisting a ticker tape dance through the magnetic plush
of anemone fingers reaching into oversized manila envelopes

(sanctified valentine
in utero extremis).

The seedy pulp of sunflowering high noons in boxed lunch offices
with redflowering sushi and lacquerware
sticking the polluted pollen of viscous heart—
epithelial kimono silk—dilating to dimensions of premature prognosis—

the broken beat of time, measured in silver teaspoons
of nauseating ether—and the siren song of drowning mermaids
        embroidering the counterfeit goldrush fringe

of stock exchanges—coin-sized overreach toward the numb vanishing point
    of decimated dollars and decapitated cents.

And Icarus minted in accolades of green—
plunging into the copperplate sea of acidic tears—waxing toward the boiling
point on the Hudson horizon of disheveled trees in Riverside Park—
of sinking suns and new moons giving new birth to the fallen

stars and the debris of night, the harlot's jewelcase flung open
        at the neon feet of commuters surging through turnstiles—
      roiling mass of Nikes and rollerblades and Evian limbs
winging home on spiked Gatorade.

Deli lights splintering

through the fluorescent eyes of the nymphomaniac caravan
needling through the needy night murmurous with the junky scrawl of graffiti

incantations rumbling through the groins of iconoclastic acolytes—

green with gangrenous envy and burning bile, the new apocalypse
squeezing through the tinfoiled undergarments of transvestites chewing on
tinsel gumwrappers and gunshot wounds—
bleeding a stigmata of spare change and jangling eyes,
begging the bony hand to cast a
jaundiced benediction of swiney

pearls twining rosary beads of perspiration through the tangled traffic of
funereal arteries oozing green blood and light through the Eustachian
tunnels and the blood-

shot eye vessels blinking on jewelstrung highways and AM radio
static crackling through the dark of flying night at Ground
Zero below sea level.

On the Prowl in the East Village

Streetwalking shades stalk each other
in stilettos and sequins; dagger eyes glint behind
the rheumy film of narcotic fatigue—

dodging round dark
corners with the perspicacity of
perspiration and fake pearls—
impeccably aligned on sagging G-strings—
for the fake swine breeding
in sanitation trucks and overflowing
dumpsters.

After all, they were castaway
snakes itching to shed scaly desiccated skins—
writhing beneath
disenchanted moons—drifting behind grimy window glass—

reflecting back the cracked dawn
hardening into hungover morning glare upon plaster-flaking walls of shivering tenements, recalling the shudder of pale orgasm; craving diner eggs and slabs of buttered toast on thick cracked plates, and muddy lukewarm coffee— egg yolk yellow streaking across oil-painted horizons.

The Exotic Dancer

She undulates a cocaine dream,
psychopomp of dry-iced
cocktails, salted
rocks &
splin-
  tered chandelier nights.

She draws rhinestone accolades—
sticky shot glass
pennies &
overstuffed dollars from hoodwinked
snakeskin wallets in crinkled

Armani pants,
lapdancing private
peek-a-boo booths of
beaded curtain tricks spilling
champagne buckets &
mirrored silver—
spitting out pomegranate
seeds from between
tiny porcelain teeth at
gargoyle stevedores
ogling painted caravans &
copping a Coptic
animadversion—

shedding flimsy wrap-
around skirts &
polyester lace bra
straps to a mere
G-string of scaly gorgon eyes
      glittering hard
       sequins
      at tassled
      ballerina
      antics

twisting a tourniquet of
trapeze tulle &
tight fishnet round &

round a flaccid drum
delirium—

spinning acrobatic
tilting a dizzy
high-rise axis toward a
levity of gyrating
Jerusalems.

Castaway snake
goddess, she
writhes hieroglyphically
beneath disenchanted moons—

her calculated striptease
catalyzes a litany of

Village junkies
plastic saints
ex-communicated *mater dolorosas*
nymphomaniacal hermaphrodites
dungeon damsels with dagger eyes &
bearded hipsters.

Queen of orgiastic limbo,
she staggers into
Grand Central Station—
vomiting a

sequence of swiney pearls,
high-strung on
cheap champagne.

The Abortion

placentae of Red Seatide trailing umbilical

[cordless]

parallel wakes carve flora of the unknown

      [deep]

fetal tissue bleeds guilt
flush and rinse amniotic

        power | plush

pulsate palpable dialectic
dilate [indeterminate] dimensions

diacritical prognosis of urinary

dialysis split-
   ting atoms   along a   long hairy   razor's edge

[Determine point of incision.

Scalpel scrapes naked
goose-
flesh.]

surgical paraphernalia dictate premature decision & ultra-

sound a song of drowning
seamaidens & swallow

sickle-
  celled moons

ripple epithelial horizons
bloom stigmata &
wild anemone

Pap smear

crustaceous blood; snatch a
sticky trinket &
feed the vultures of time
cancer from the diaphanous
damsel's heart &

clitoridec-
tomy
of

cutaneous membrane
(*speculum in saecorum*)

twisted DNA
  helix weave
    chromo-
     somes
      [grid-
        lock]

diametric | opposition

race along cardinal axes—mutate a Petri

dish of blackbirds mingling the clink of tarnished coins in abortion clinic cash registers the clatter of high heels ricocheting down mimetic corridors of memory drowning in formaldehyde & stench of oblivion.

Menstruation at Fifty

Menstruation at fifty remains
a vital possibility—stretching the elastic limit of statistical averages—despite
Anne Sexton's celebration of the gynecological phenomenon at merely forty.

So, as my tribute to her,
and to all the women of the world for whom she wrote "In Celebration of My Uterus":

I celebrate this monthly event—flowering red streamers in clear water when I relieve myself—resisting the flush into oblivion this rich life-giving blood—I gaze entranced by the fertile possibility unfolding origami petals, one by one, confirming itself each month.

Will this be the last?
Are these hot flashes?
I spring forward with DST—my head a perspiring hothouse flower.

My toned, caffeinated, sinewed, vitamin-enriched
womansbody sings:

Praised be my gynecology, its menstrual apparatus
        my ovaries
     fallopian tubes
          breasts
          cervix
          uterus

and all that lies in-between

cardinal points (epithelial and epigrammatic)—
cancer-free and running clockwise toward months that will secrete their intentions, red origami petals paling.

Hot Flashing

Heat rises to the red
zenith point, my
body a thermometer—
sudden skip of
Fahrenheit degrees—
waxing into clean,
empty months,
flush upon flush—
mounting into my head,
an overblown rose
perspiring anxiety;
drenching bed linen—
epithelial stretch of bone-
colored tissue, and
moons vanishing
in sickle-celled skies.

Porcelain Lady

I remember her porcelain fragility—the way she handled her neurosis
carefully like medieval embroidery, or Ming china, her eggshell
lining skin shot through with Botox injections and other

kinds of invective that hadn't been invented yet. Her alcoholic
fingers stapled photocopy askew: she couldn't align the ruler with
her hemline to see who measured up to whom
despite her six-foot height.

We were caged birds of a different
species from each other singing shrill ditties for the supper that never
came to us at the Interlibrary Loan (ILL)
Department we cohabited.

We wasted time on the clock begging the hairy
prince to come to us like a good Neanderthal in a silver G-string.

And maybe he did come for us to perform the Chippendale's
dance behind locked doors, gyrating voyeuristic
Vaseline moves in skewed Manhattan moonlight. Yet she remains

for me the porcelain lady with her raucous
neuroses: She gawks at me from behind the torn
lace years—mistress of bitchy vodka moods.

Today, I'm sorry I never knew anything about the rain she saw behind eyelids
shuttered against the storm that bothered her—
when she told me about her hairy pedophilic uncle. Perhaps she

saw him standing in the moonglare behind
my back. At least we know he shouldn't have reached into the pubic
spaces of her body like parks closed after Sunday dark. After all these years,
perhaps we

can escape the ILL cage we cohabited, once upon a time when the prince
came to us in the scintillating regalia of respective desires for liberation from
our father the hairy ape and the luciferian angel of antediluvian mercy and
elusive catharsis behind moonshot G-strung eyelids.

And perhaps the caged birds will sing again and won't fall
off their perches into narcissistic sunlight. And perhaps
an invective has been invented for Ming china and we can dig our way to
the other side of the moon.

The Exotic Dance Club Patron

I saw him,
sitting alone,
at the Kit Kat Klub bar, his back
turned toward the vast tinseled stage where

pale, young,
vulnerable dancers
shed plaid wrap-
around skirts
and polyester
bras. He was

my dream guy
in the underworld of live
adult entertainment
on W. 43rd St. near
Times Square; between Hell's
Kitchen and the Garment District.

Unlikely hipster
patron, his dark
eyes gazed at melting ice
cubes swirling in
the unreplenished
glass before him. I

broke his trance—
a disarmed
enchantress, cock-
tail waitress novice;
I'd forgotten
to order the designated
overpriced crap
champagne from the
frowning bartender
who'd asked me,

"What would you like to drink?"
—the patron being expected
to pay, and I, his pimped

server to follow the scripted sequence: sip, spit, smile—
the champagne being orally
transferred to the frosted
glass simulating water chaser—
as though champagne needs to be chased by anything other than its own effervescence.

We'd planned a tryst,
to meet up, after I'd clocked out of
the Kit Kat Klub. I
didn't bother to claim
the sordid night's wages, and he
didn't show up. Instead,

I'd remembered him,
        a shadow shivering along Times Square sidewalks,
                      blinking into neon graffiti—

an angelic scrawl across smoggy New York City skies.

The "Four Stages of Eroticism" (Eve, Helen, Mary, Sophia)

1. Eve

Eve! Her fig leaf

        flutters away—pubic transience, and reek of sin.

Garlic nymph!

Unblemished belly,
bowl of wild wheat,
immaculate bulge
      of woman's flesh, Adam's

ribbed condom, castaway
      snakeskin slithering away, shriveled, among palm trees,
           hissing, heavy with milk and sorrow, fading into
                the dapple of fallen apples—
naked, long-haired Mother,
apple of God's unblinking gold eye,
she gags on dust
flaking off the serpent's

      soft delectable underbelly—
          rising like bread in the ovens of misogyny.

2. Helen

Helen! Her fair beacon brow
      sends off ships in hazardous directions.

Helen! Her feet, unsandaled, step on
      scorpions in the desert of our thirst.

Helen! Pale dove,
Her mouth full of olives
Her eyes plucked pearls from the Aegean Sea

Her hair a shimmering net—
      capturing minnows, piranhas—
         grimacing oysters spitting out grainy pearls
            for the swine groveling for eye candy at her heavy,
embroidered hem.

Helen! She is the lost civilization,
Now, a caryatid,

carrying the weight of lovely misogyny.

3. Mary

Mary! The snake writhes beneath her unshod
        feet, vomiting dust like an overused vacuum cleaner hose—
                coughing up the debris of the B.C. centuries (fattened
centaurs).

Mary! The pearl-eyed swine gag on withered fig leaves and desiccated
                snakeskin. The light is her kind friend, her
        veils superfluous annuities.

Mary! She kneels beneath
        the slivery new moon, God's
castaway fingernail paring.

The Annunciation ruptured
her vermillion shield—cremated her shivering bones, the burning
                sensation immaculately coalescing into a

squeaky "Yes," a church mouse caught
in misogyny's trap door.

4. Sophia

Sophia! Unscratched diamond,
consummate abstraction;
scrubbed windowpane
of the ecstatic soul—pinnacle
of Jung's "four stages," laureled
without Apollo's muscled, raping arm;
wise serpents gather in the folds
of her flowing robes, breeding
circumspectly—shedding scaly
skin without the weight of sin, or
pearly, candied swine eyes, or
polluted ozone veils, or
broken chastity belts—

just purity,
among overblown lilies.

Votive candles melt at her Gnostic altar—
waxing into mandala light.

Bivalve

Norman Bates &
his mother are
the white heterosexual male's
bivalve brain parts, symbiotic
prototypes of derailed American

dreams (and
not only the wet, or plastic
variety) because

every man wants
to be his own mother
without the hassle of
donning a grey wig and a faded
calico dress—of

having to fuck
her as though she were
the blind sphinx
of untimely oracles. Also,

because the uroboric
urge to cross-dress and be
that (M)other is normalized
bait for misogyny.

Realia

Wavy cascade of mousy brown hair, exhibit
at the Lilly Library, invites voyeuristic
"peanut-crunching" crowds to gawk awkwardly—shorn from the
[actual] head that was

Sylvia Plath's. From papery catacombs, the realia object was
resurrected, whispering her abjected
name—Lady Lazarus, her
curvilinear remnant
fusing the golden ash, the slippery
          mirror, the Japanese moon, the paper sky—crinkling into

bone-colored preservation tissue. Castaway
snaky DNA strand of a goddess smiling
hieroglyphically at her

accomplished striptease; she
devours ether—vomiting peanut
shells, the stink of formaldehyde clinging to her
"old whore petticoats."

The Iconization of Rosa Parks

When they tucked her away in a bed
of roses in the Capitol Rotunda,
did the Republican thorns
scrape away her dignity,
the color of red sea
ignominy—scratch out
eyes that no longer saw
a divided America?

When she refused to rise from her sticky
seat, did she think she would be
queen of the Civil Rights movement
in the humiliating carbon monoxide
stench that clung to her
heavy askew skirt,
seamstress stitching together the
arbitrarily missing pieces of our divided,
wounded, gunshot America and her long-armed
sons tilling the earth for the good salt
beneath the soiled bedrock
and her large-breasted daughters
bending their heads to the blowing storm?

She rises now from her seat
of ignominy in terribly
scarlet glory—into the historical ether,
to the graffiti of noise
behind tombstone
eyelids—an articulate icon
that never spoke,
nor raised a dark fist
against adamant storm clouds.

She is the ironic democracy
silent iconoclast
superintendent of dreams,
attended by servile roses.

Life Drawing

Straining optical nerves beyond limits of the [immediately] visible—the life drawing model is squarely positioned before her, an immobile granite sphinx of luminous flesh—a challenging assignment—every fiber of the artist's body pulsates outward from beneath

skin's thick epithelial lining and its pointillistic pores—steadily guiding the disciplined hand's 4B pencil stub, converting molecules of lead into curvilinear lineaments on the unsullied sketchbook page… [She feels the film of grey scum already seeping out of her pores, already coating her tense body straining toward that unblinking fleshy sphinx].

She draws the lines, then, blurs, and smears them (again and again); dragging shadows into their proper places; always trying to maintain perspective without undue manipulation [of objects outside the frame she is working within].

So tentative at first, and then, so boldly obvious with stroke upon stroke accumulating layers of charcoal grey emphasis—covering the same ground.

The figure emerges from the sheet of paper as though it were always meant to be there exactly, a tentative smudge boldly outlined—a grey voluptuous shadow—projected outward from the artist's own body perspiring scum pointilistically.

Speaking for Edvard Munch's *The Sin*

I am your sin,
long-haired woman
coiling serpent
praises round
your throat: I cling
to you like the fragrance
you wear compulsively
without my consent.
I am the carbon
monoxide your rattling
ribcage exhales; the jeweled
oxymoron; thorn in the flesh
of your Achilles heel,
your frailty housed
in treacherous nunnery
dark after vespers
evaporate a catacomb
stench of bones &
memories of how
you masturbated on full
moon nights like a silly
bleached vampire.

Darling, I am
your wide-eyed sin—
growing unkempt
secrets behind your
eyelids, the dirt in your
fingernails, the piss in your
pants, the garlic
nymph reeking
formaldehyde.

Lazarus

Her eyes glinted hard blue bits
of Indiana summer sky
as she aggressively combed the circular clearance
rack—round and round the
numbers spun by—25% 50% 75% off

original prices—major markdown to the vanishing point of infinitesimal decimal places
> growing gargantuan greed like green moss and
> decimated daisies in the daily
> crevices of the consumerist American dream
> promising us biggest bargains.

Plastic sales tags swung in the interstices indicating size
> demarcations [XS, S, M, L, XL]—I struggled to freeze

the spinning rack at XS/S—she resisted in the opposite
circular direction toward L/XL—endless tug-of-war—
> hangers scraping discordant concertos—a carousel of

ghastly color and synthetic fabric—flimsily stitched
> together garments hanging

askew, forlorn like the skins of baggy ghosts flapping and begging to be inhabited
> immediately—to be purchased at 75% off and stuffed
> into plastic shopping bags with neatly stapled return
> receipts—to lie once again forgotten in our overstuffed,
> oversized, suburban closets spewing out a predictable
> barrage of garage sales in the backyards of Bloomington,
> Indiana—Lazarus resurrected endlessly.

Kroger

Bike-rush to Kroger—
in my employee-discounted Indiana University fitness leggings and Target sports bra—for $4.99 Barefoot Pinot Grigio and sushi (only if 1 pkg. costs less than $6.00)—culminated in braking @ the bike rack before a window glass reflection that pleased me

—wind blowing long fine hair in one direction—freshly shampooed and conditioned with Matrix Biolage hair care products, styled by Connie @ Perfect Illusion—I felt like a supermodel (despite my XS petite size)—the sun and the wind and my strength merging and coursing through my caffeine-fueled body—pulsating outwardly from sun-saturated bodywashed pores... Directly juxtaposed with this glass reflection just around the

redbrick corner with the sign reading:

> "No
> Loitering
> Or
> Panhandling"

stood a woman with chunky ankles, askew skirts, wispy faded hair pulled back in a slovenly ponytail, whose gaze met mine behind my Nine West shades (exorbitant plexiglass barrier between ourselves). I U-locked my Trek bike:

the woman seemed like she wanted to shrink into herself—possibly disappear around some remote corner that only she could access—where she could loiter or panhandle for a sympathetic smile without shame. And indeed she did

(disappear) the moment I glanced up from my U-lock—an unlikely grey specter in the south side of Bloomington, Indiana—as improbable as my own reflected window glass self—shimmering arbitrary fragments of economic value.

The Doll

Saddled with a doll,
hard, slippery, oversized, celluloid thing—
no purpose for it, besides staring,
equally wide-eyed, into its blinking
eyes, fringed with black
plastic eyelashes.

Celluloid weight,
aircraft encumbrance—shoved into the overhead
bin, replica of the hollow girl-child
I was, shoveling strawberry ice cream into
my cold mouth
with a tiny wood spoon
   at Haneda Airport. Then, the nauseating descent toward JFK International—

a pillow on my churning tummy
filling loose seatbelt space, making up for
     the airborne difference. Surely, the doll was rolling around, vomiting turbulence—

till the aircraft landed a serene,
    intact origami crane gliding across celluloid runways.

Duck, Duck, Goose

Round and round, the boys they ran—
around the circle of girls in demure pigtails,
and tight braids—impatient to be goosed,
to receive the golden egg, prize without King
Midas' compromising touch. The
boys skirted the issue—attempting to tag each
other outside the squirming circle of
bored girls, nurturing goose eggs—pulling each
other's pigtails, laughing, squealing, knowing
there never would be a breach in their golden circle—
an endless game with no winner—
endless chase after the constipated goose.

"Wanted"

That smiling brunette, so
unlike a mugshot;
the camera was her friend—
its flash carving out for her a
haloed whitespace.

"WANTED: Patricia Campbell Hearst,"
read the 1974 B/W poster at the
Amsterdam Ave. P.O. near
Columbia University, the decade
when I'd learned to read, a gawking
uniformed first-grader at
St. Hilda's & St. Hugh's School. Patty

Hearst morphed into my RTS symptom
after 2001 till I felt like a badass
white woman, my head a scrambled egg,
imagining a mannequin wielding a
machine gun—ripping up tawdry
marquees with scathing gunfire—
tortuous machinations contorting torsos into askew
positions—feeding stale bread crumbs
to the vulturous media. Over the years,

my scrambled head coalesced, bloomed,
a gold chrysanthemum—and the SLA
symbol wriggled into its proper archived place—
a castrated 7-headed cobra.

Grandma and the Devil

Pea soup projectile—
the only *Exorcist* scene
Grandma mentioned during our
lunch at the Meguro
train station restaurant near
Shiroganedai, Tokyo. I

could've lost it (the
Okosama lunch)
and developed
an aversion for pea soup,
if only, I'd known
that Grandma could've
pinned the tail on
the Devil's cleft
behind, even as she
solemnly slurped
her noodles. I'd

wanted her to be
the consoling authority
figure, not merely
stating the obvious—
that the vomit
scene was "gross"
("*Kimochi ga
warui*"). I'd wanted her
to exorcise my ten-
year-old girl terror
without the diegetic
death. Instead, she was

the grey, wispy
soul guardian after my
parents' divorce, her
bones a bundle
of chopsticks behind
finely wrinkled skin, her
shriveled, flattened-out
breasts beneath
kimono folds

castaway Japanese
snakeskin. And so,

the Devil slithered away with the desiccated years—
        vomiting dust like an overworked vacuum cleaner hose,
              and Grandma became a memory, folded away,
like a grey, moth-eaten kimono
in my mind's overstuffed linen closet.

Lily of the Valley

Drop tiny white clusters of
angel heads—modestly
innocent like baby's breath,

but poisonous. Red berries dangle
delight & venom (bleeding heart
droplets) the scarlet

        side of the madonna |

whore dichotomy.

The Rejected Daffodil

Yellow starburst
so unexpectedly soon,
lovely consequence
of indoor relocation—
the daffodil's more vibrantly
golden cohorts having been
seized by my girlish,
hair-flowing neighbors
crying, "Spring!"

The rejected daffodil's
yellow head had drooped as
though ashamed of its unworth
to be plucked
by spring-greedy hands. Its

sunlit cohort crowd
had beckoned me to snip
translucent stems,
staunch invisible roots buried
in frozen soil—grey gravitational pull
from unkempt backyard to cinderblock apartment.

The lone
rejected bloom
(literal wall
flower)
was all
that had remained
    after the neighborly daffodil raid—like culling sunshine by the armloads,
        unlikely promise of viability, greenly tinged as though sick with
envy—

before the overnight starburst at my Virgin Mary shrine and accolades of gold
smiled—
                miles beyond the backyard of the vacant house next
door.

IN v. LDS

When he stepped across the
dilapidated threshold—ruptured
the screened window, did he
see the scrawny girl in the woman
disheveled with sleep? No, instead,
he blindfolded the stars, and taped the
mouths of the flowers shut. I

watched him unfasten
his pants. Will he
spend 7 years on good behavior,
masturbating with the memory
of how he raped me
with the fantasy of consensus—
pulling arms and chairs into askew
positions of compromise? After all, he

dug himself a cinderblock
hole, and buried the deed
with a burglary conviction
quite euphemistically.

It suddenly occurred to me that
"Rape is redemption for woman,"
as I read Sylvia Plath's *Unabridged
Journals* among the wild lilies
at the Cox Arboretum, July 2001;
how Sylvia longed to be
raped by the sun [that killed
Icarus]. This was all

before the done fact [16 years
before #MeToo] when I
accessed the information
that rape was a 1:4 statistic
of namelessly shamed women in the United
States of America. After the fall

into logistical knowledge,
I understood that the
Monroe County Prosecutor
could neither touch nor mend the bruised
mouths and sunken breasts of these
statistical women going the hard way
of nunnery stones, begging us to read

between the squiggly lines
of sex offender registries. Since then, I

compulsively use the Odyssey
Case Management System to search for updated offender information, catatonic architectures of consensus coalescing and dissolving, reminding me that justice was

truncated in the evacuated
courtrooms of Bloomington, Indiana.

#MeToo

I am a #MeToo woman—flowering grit, scrubbed
  down marrow, phoenix ash resurrected—my head a glowing chrysanthemum moon,
     petaled and papered, unsplintered chandelier.

The #MeToo women form an endless chain of unleashed outraged voices—
serpentine
  cyber-trail
     shrill, gruff, plaintive, bittersweet, raucous harmony—

I am
  one of them, dodging misogynistic bullets,
     disingenuous catcalls purring   obscene whispers.

The Ragdoll

Not merely stuffed away in a
claustrophobic cradle in a cobwebbed
attic, but kidnapped
instead [as Gregory Corso says:
"A favorite doll
knows the pain of a child's farewell"].

Ginger yarn hair and black
button eyes; tiny white pinafore edged
with eyelet lace; I'd named my ragdoll
"Charlotte" after Laura Ingalls
Wilder's doll.   "She is

our customers' favorite item," I was
informed at that Newport RI giftshop
where the doll rang up more

than $50.00 on AMEX credit
on that cash register overflowing
receipts and green pennies, but that was not
the point

when the rapist took her as a
souvenir of his needless
accomplishment (unlike other
bedroom paraphernalia to

obstruct justice)—haphazard thing
that stood in for the raped
woman herself, the

cost of the doll itemized
in the unclaimed $1,230.00 restitution
total, a bloodless turnip.

Piano Burning

Why burn a piano
when other things can use
the burning more effectively?

Vacant houses, biohazardous and
possibly haunted by lead molecules
swirling pointillistically

into toxic ghosts; or
love letters, anachronistic,
outliving love object memories—collapsing into fragile
origami tents. Flaming chords,

discordant keys—scorch nostrils
with needless apocalypse.

Icarus Redux

Green roses bloomed for Icarus
beneath his pasty heels
when they hit the Aegean seawaves
with a vociferous splash.

He morphed into the flipped
bird at high noon when he gave the finger
to the sun god Helios—falling out of the burning sky—a charred piece
   of debris, floating like a dust mote, or

a waxy   speck   in the blinking

eye.

His ego waxed as the sun waxed shedding
hot golden tears—feathers sadly drifting from the cunningly wrought osier
framework of
      synthetic wings—upon the oily surface of the sea, an interminable
canvas of sloppy
      experiments, choppy with roiling acrylic paint.

He then became a work of art (however
crappily executed)—gawked at in museum galleries,
featured in poems by W. H. Auden and William Carlos Williams (albeit
to illustrate such things as the massive indifference of teeming human life—
busy as geeky ants, and almost as blind).

He even stood in for suicide Sylvia
and all the other heroic icons who failed
to die the normal geriatric way.

So, when green roses bloomed for Icarus,
green became the iconic color *par excellence*; oxidized copper pennies
became the tarnished currency—circulating corrosive envy and burning
bile—and Icarus was minted in accolades of green.

What mortician of high noon can reverse this process of oxidization, restore
the clean gold face of the sun, the wings of our Copernican darling—
accomplish the mission of Daedalus without unseemly detriment?

Green roses bloomed for all of us
when Icarus fell

from the
sky.

Additional Acknowledgments

The poems in *Icarus Burning* coalesced during the eighteen years since 9-11, the apocalyptic day when the American dream was decimated overnight into shards and fragments scintillating in the sun that melted the wings of Icarus. Since then, the dream has been resurrected from Ground Zero ash like a mad disheveled phoenix, proving that some marrow steely part of ourselves remains intact even after that surreal nightmare of improbable apocalypse. Thus, these poems are like the offspring of that Ground Zero phoenix, Icarus resprouting wings, soaring toward the altitudes at which the ozone layer remains intact in rainbow colors.

And so, for the possibility of these poems, I thank many wonderful people. A million thanks to the organizers, instructors, and scholarship sponsors for the Indiana University Writers' Conference, who encouraged me to develop my craft. These wonderful individuals are: Amy Locklin, Laura Otto, Jacqueline Jones LaMon, and Neil Perry; Marilyn Chin, Ruth Ellen Kocher, Catherine Bowman, and Heather McHugh; David Wojahn, Laura Leffers Bybee, and Allison Joseph. Their encouragement, guidance, and sponsorship have enabled these poems to bloom.

Thanks duly go to the Artsgarden in Indianapolis; and Soma, Boxcar Books & Community Center, The Runcible Spoon Café & Restaurant, Rachael's Café, The Switchyard, Blue Studio Gallery, Player's Pub, and The Bishop, in Bloomington, Indiana, for authorizing and hosting spoken word performances for some of these poems. My thanks extend to the Writers Guild at Bloomington for sponsoring some of these performances.

While I thank the shades of Allen Ginsberg, Gregory Corso, Sylvia Plath, and Anne Sexton for their inspiration, I also thank the more palpable beings in my life since 2004 for the friendship that grounded my poems in the concrete confessional stuff of life: Tony Brewer, JL Kato, Matt O'Neill, Ian Girdley, Dennis Ray Powell Jr., Darcy Fisher, John Isbell (Fish), Kerry Anderson, Kathleen Clark-Perez, Claudio Perez, Joshua Byron, and all the "angelheaded hipsters" of Bloomington who migrated from Three-Headed Dog at Sun-Ra to the Ream, Magnetic South, Russian Recording, and beyond.

Most precious thanks to my mother, Dr. Toyoko Yoshida, for endless support, encouragement, and love. She is the immaculately bleached bone of the phoenix, of which I remain the delicate steely offshoot.

Thank you all for all these years when green roses bloomed quietly in our unkempt backyards.

About the Author

Born in Tokyo, Japan, **Hiromi Yoshida** became a naturalized citizen of the United States of America in 2014. Because she grew up in the Columbia University neighborhood of Manhattan's upper westside, where Beat Generation writers had gravitated, her affinity with them is particularly strong. Recognized as one of Bloomington's "finest and most outspoken poets," her *Green Roses Bloom for Icarus* is a semi-finalist selection for the 2018 Wilder Series Poetry Book Prize. She is also a three-time winner of Indiana University Writers' Conference poetry awards.

While studying for a PhD in English, Hiromi Yoshida published *Joyce & Jung: The "Four Stages of Eroticism" in A Portrait of the Artist as a Young Man*. Having outlined the psychosexual trajectory for Stephen Dedalus's achievement of lyric authority for *Joyce & Jung*, she decided to become a poet, the identity she had wanted to consolidate, and the profession she had wanted to practice, since her childhood years in Jack Kerouac's former neighborhood. Shortly after that decision had coalesced, "Icarus Burning," her debut poem, was published in *Bathtub Gin* in 2002. Since then, her poems have been published in various literary journals and magazines in both print and electronic format. Her publication success was particularly notable in 2015 when she published as many as eleven poems; "IN v. LDS" was nominated for a Sundress Best of the Net award; and she was featured in *The Rain, Party, & Disaster Society*.

Hiromi Yoshida's literary analysis has also been published in *Plath Profiles*, and she has curated an exhibition at the Lilly Library, *The "Big Strip Tease" of Sylvia Plath*. Having earned a Master of Arts degree in English from Fordham University, and a Master of Library Science degree with a Rare Books and Manuscripts Librarianship specialization from Indiana University Bloomington, she now teaches American literature, and haiku writing, for the award-winning VITAL program at the Monroe County Public Library.

In response to the 2016 presidential election outcome, Hiromi Yoshida organized the *Poets 4 Unity* monthly reading series to showcase Bloomington's diverse voices and to build solidarity. She was a featured poet at events that include *Speaking from the Middle: An Evening with Asian American Writers*, a reading celebrating the twentieth-year inception of the Asian Culture Center at Indiana University Bloomington; *Peace at the Intersection of Justice: Nagasaki Vigil*, at the Monroe County Courthouse Square; and the *Spoken Word Stage* at the Fourth Street Festival of the Arts and Crafts in Bloomington. She has also contributed to *Poetry On Demand*, sponsored by the Writers Guild at Bloomington, and has served on Lotus Festival committees since 2012. Her collage works, with titles such as *Icarus Ekphrasis* and *The World After the Fall of Icarus*, have been exhibited in Bloomington.